Be the Best at Science

Rebecca Rissman

Chicago, Illinois

www.capstonepub.com
Visit our website to find out more information about Heinemann-Raintree books.

To order:

☎ Phone 800-747-4992

💻 Visit www.capstonepub.com to browse our catalog and order online.

Edited by Rebecca Rissman, Dan Nunn, and Adrian Vigliano
Designed by Joanna Malivoire
Original illustrations © Capstone Global Library Ltd.
Picture research by Ruth Blair
Production by Alison Parsons
Originated by Capstone Global Library
Printed in China by CTPS

16 15 14 13 12
10 9 8 7 6 5 4 3 2 1

Library of Congress Cataloging-in-Publication Data
Rissman, Rebecca.
  Be the best at science / Rebecca Rissman.—1st ed.
      p. cm.—(Top tips)
  Includes bibliographical references and index.
  ISBN 978-1-4109-4766-6 (hb)—ISBN 978-1-4109-4771-0 (pb) 1. Science—Juvenile literature. I. Title.
  Q163.R53 2013
  500—dc23   2011043937

Acknowledgments
The author and publishers are grateful to the following for permission to reproduce copyright material: Shutterstock pp. 5 (© Mat Hayward), 7 (© wavebreakmedia ltd), 9 (© James Steidl), 11 (© Skripko Ievgen), 13 (© Tspider), 15 (© Dmitriy Shironosov), 17 (© taelove7), 17 (© Scott Sanders), 18 (© darkgreenwolf), 19 (© Yurchyks), 19 (© darkgreenwolf), 19 (© Ilya Andriyanov), 21 (© Glenda M. Powers), 23 (© Cheryl Casey), 24 (© Monkey Business Images), 27 (© oorka), 29 (© Symbiot), 30 (© Carlos E. Santa Maria). Background and design features reproduced with the permission of Shutterstock.

Cover photograph reproduced with the permission of Shutterstock and Shutterstock/© notkoo.

We would like to thank Nancy Harris for her invaluable help in the preparation of this book.

Every effort has been made to contact copyright holders of any material reproduced in this book. Any omissions will be rectified in subsequent printings if notice is given to the publisher.

Some words are shown in bold, **like this**. You can find out what they mean by looking in the glossary.

Contents

Get Going!. 4

Use the Scientific Method 6

Don't Miss a Step! 8

Question This!. 10

Observe It! .12

Make Your Guess! 14

Pay Attention!. 16

Measure It! .18

Keeping Count 20

Get the Picture! 22

Draw a Conclusion!. 24

Using Mnemonics 26

Study Like a Pro!. 28

Dream Big! .30

Glossary. 31

Find Out More 32

Index 32

Get Going!

People use science every day to do all types of things. But sometimes science can seem tricky. Don't let that stop you! Learning a few simple tricks can make even the biggest science **experiment** more fun!

Top Tip

Get going! The more science you do, the easier it will get. Spend 15 minutes every day asking scientific questions. Try to do scientific experiments, too!

5

Use the Scientific Method

We use a set of steps called the **scientific method** to answer questions or solve problems in science. Using the scientific method makes sure that the answer, or **outcome**, of an **experiment** is something you can trust.

Question	ask what you would like to know about a topic
Observe	learn what you can about your topic
Hypothesize	make an informed guess about the answer to your question
Experiment	test your hypothesis or guess
Record Data	take notes on what happens
Draw a Conclusion	decide whether your hypothesis was correct

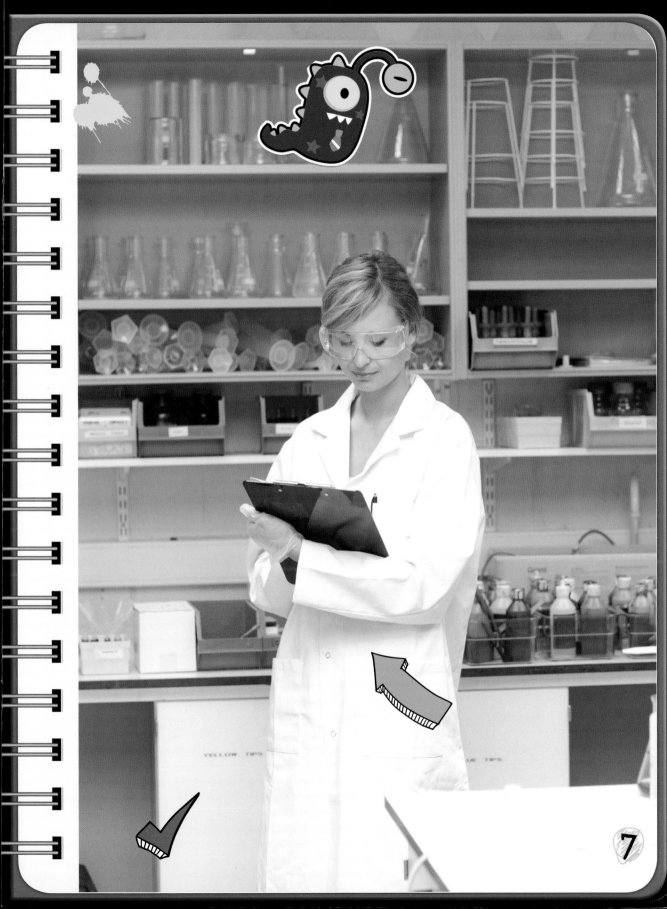

Don't Miss a Step!

The **scientific method** is very helpful to scientists. But you need to remember all of the steps!

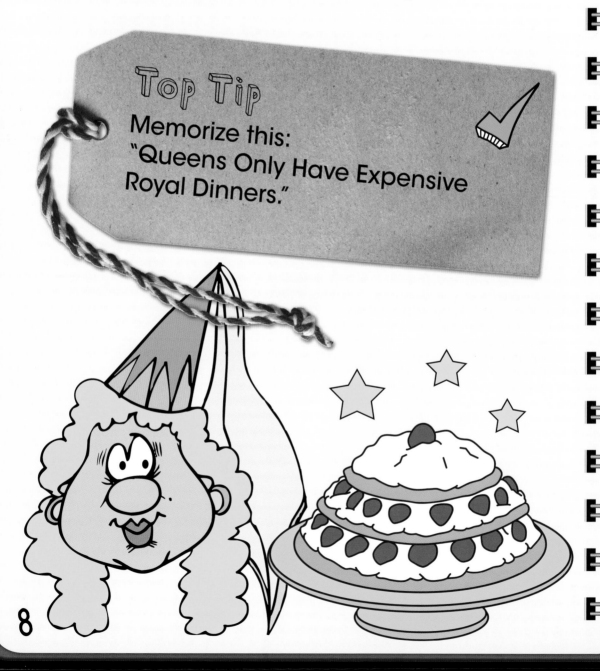

Top Tip

Memorize this: "Queens Only Have Expensive Royal Dinners."

Test That Tip!

Each word in the sentence starts with the first letter of the words in the scientific method:

Queens: **Question**

Only: **Observe**

Have: **Hypothesize**

Expensive: **Experiment**

Royal: **Record Data**

Dinners: **Draw a Conclusion**

Question This!

Asking the right type of questions is very important in science.

Top Tip

You should be able to test your question by changing one **variable**, or thing, to find your answer. Only ask questions that require one change in your **experiment**, or test.

Got it!

Test That Tip!

You wonder how long it would take someone to bicycle 1 mile. Which question works better?

How long does it take to bike 1 mile?

Or

How long does it take for Juanita to ride her bicycle 1 mile?

Observe It!

The second step of the **scientific method** reminds us to **observe**, or look closely at, our topic. This might mean doing **research** to learn more about the topic.

Top Tip

When observing your topic, make a KWL chart:

- Things I *Know*

- Things I *Want* to know

- Things I've *Learned*

Bikes	
Things I *know*	
Things I *want* to know	
Things I've *learned*	

Make Your Guess!

After you have **observed** your topic, it's time to make your **hypothesis**, or best guess. For example, "If Juanita rides her bike downhill, then her speed will increase" is a hypothesis. Remember, it doesn't matter if your hypothesis is right or wrong. The results of your experiment will still be valuable!

Top Tip

Many good hypotheses fit into the "If, Then" pattern.

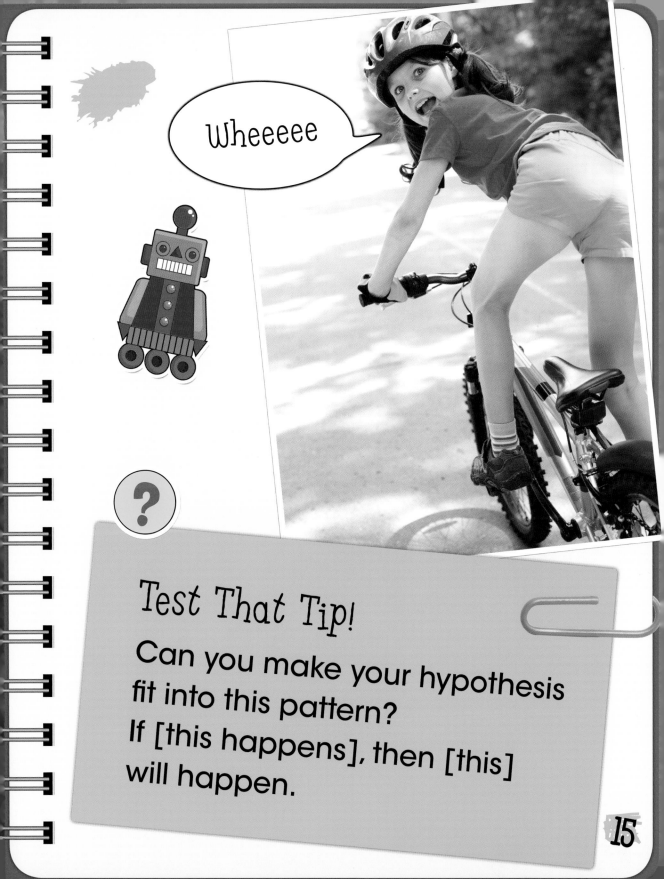

Wheeeee

Test That Tip!

Can you make your hypothesis fit into this pattern?

If [this happens], then [this] will happen.

15

Pay Attention!

While you do your science **experiment**, or test, remember to pay attention. You will need to take notes and look at everything that happens. If you don't **record**, or write down your results, no one will know what you were able to prove!

Top Tip

Pay attention to **details** when you take notes. Always:

- Record the date of your experiment.
- Write down any measurements you take.
- Record the materials you use.
- If possible, take photos.

December 14th

It takes 30 seconds for Juanita to ride from the curb to the tree.

Measure It!

Science **experiments**, or tests, often ask you to measure different things. You need to remember which tools are used for which measurements!

Top Tip

Use a scale—to measure weight

Use a ruler or yardstick—to measure height

Use a thermometer—to measure temperature

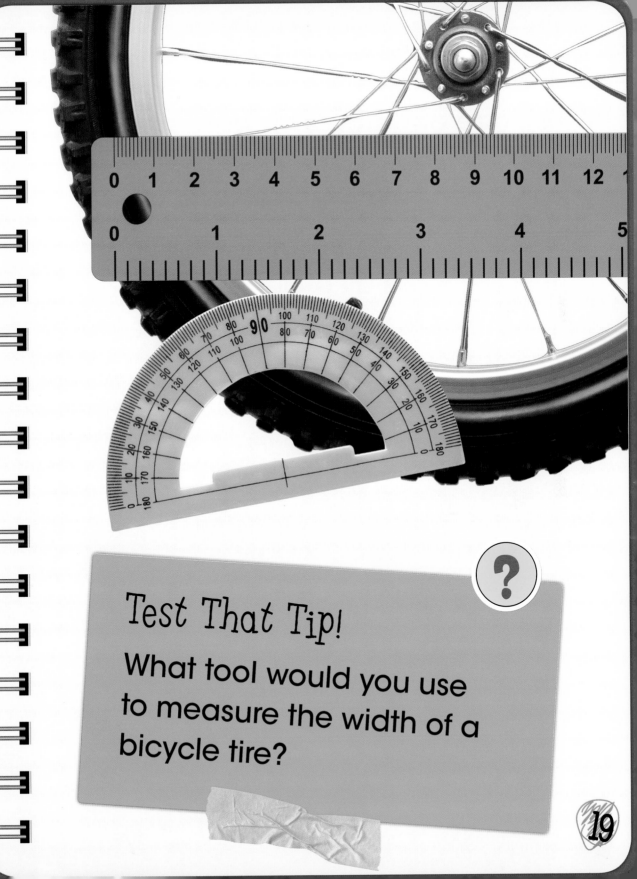

Test That Tip!

What tool would you use to measure the width of a bicycle tire?

Keeping Count

Some **experiments**, or tests, have results that you can count or measure. When doing this type of experiment, remember to **record**, or write down all of your results.

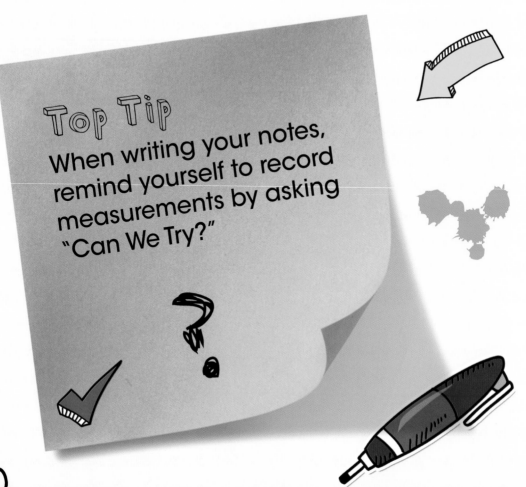

Top Tip

When writing your notes, remind yourself to record measurements by asking "Can We Try?"

Test That Tip!

Each word in the question starts with the first letter of different measuring words.

Can: Count

We: Weigh

Try: Time how long something takes

Get the Picture!

Some **experiments**, or tests, do not have results that you can count or measure. For example, the following **hypothesis** cannot be measured in numbers: "If Juanita exercises before she rides her bike, then her face turns red." To **record** what happens in these experiments, you need to:

• Draw a picture.

• Take a photograph.

• Write a description.

Top Tip
Take careful notes!

Test That Tip!

Which is a better description of the outcome of this experiment: Juanita's nose and forehead were pink, and her cheeks turned dark red.

Or

Her face was red.

Phew...

Draw a Conclusion!

Your conclusion is a summary of how your **experiment** results either showed that your hypothesis was correct or incorrect.

Don't worry if your experiment didn't prove your hypothesis! It still helped you to learn something!

Top Tip

Don't forget to share your results! There are many fun ways to teach others what you've learned, such as:

A video

A school report

A science poster

Using Mnemonics

Science teaches us amazing things about the world around us. But sometimes there can be a lot to remember. **Mnemonics** are tools we can use to remember things. Page 8 of this book uses a mnemonic to remember the steps in the **scientific method**.

"Queens Only Have Expensive Royal Dinners."

Top Tip

Make your own mnemonics as you study science!

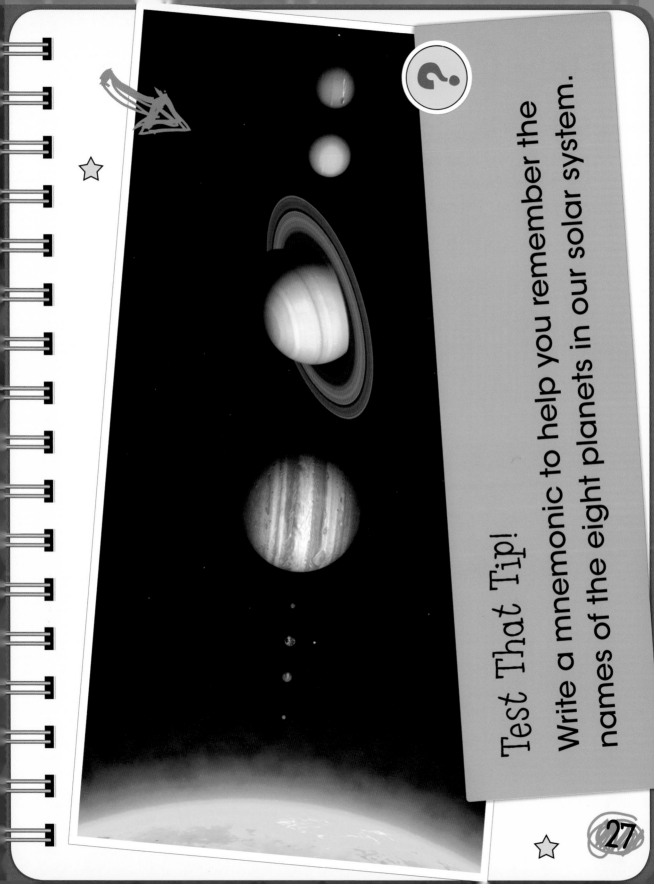

Test That Tip!

Write a mnemonic to help you remember the names of the eight planets in our solar system.

Study Like a Pro!

Set yourself up to succeed by practicing these tips when you do your homework or study.

Top Tip

Before you get to work, always:

➤ Eat a healthy snack

➤ Turn off the television

➤ Make sure you have all the supplies you need:

- textbook
- scrap paper
- pencil and eraser

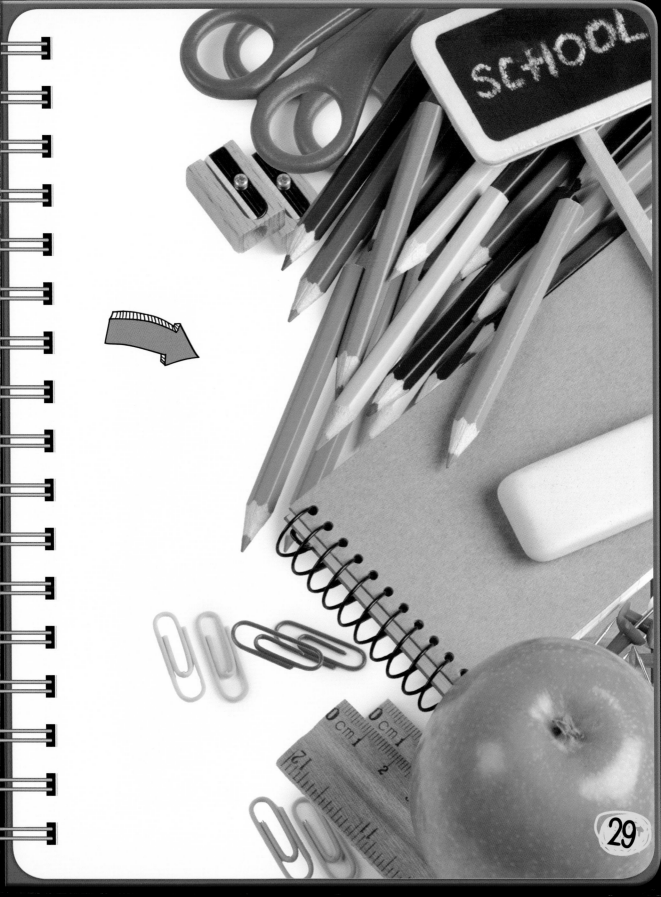

Dream Big!

Remember, learning science can be useful in many ways as you grow up! You can use it to ask questions and learn more about the world. Or you might use it in your job as a teacher, doctor, or pilot!

Glossary

data information collected, such as facts, statistics, or observations

detail small part

experiment controlled test to learn something

hypothesize (hypothesis) educated guess about the outcome of an experiment

mnemonic interesting or fun way to remember something

observe to carefully watch or notice

outcome final product or end result

record write down

research careful investigation into something

scientific method way to do an experiment. The scientific method has 6 steps.

variable part of a scientific experiment that can change

Find Out More

Books

Bender, Lionel. *Science Safety* (Being Careful). Mankato, MN: Picture Window Books, 2007.

Somervill, Barbara A. *Studying and Tests* (School Project Survival Guides). Chicago: Heinemann Library, 2009.

Taylor-Butler, Christine. *My Science Investigation* (Series). Chicago: Heinemann Library, 2012.

Internet sites

Facthound offers a safe, fun way to find Internet sites related to this book. All of the sites on Facthound have been researched by our staff.

Here's all you do:

Visit *www.facthound.com*

Type in this code: 9781410947666

Index

conclusions 6, 9, 24

data 6, 9
details 16

experiments 5, 6, 9, 10, 14, 16, 18, 20, 22, 24

hypotheses 6, 9, 14, 15, 22, 24

KWL charts 12–13

measurements 16, 18, 19, 20–21
mnemonics 8–9, 20–21, 26, 27

observation 6, 9, 12–13

practice 5, 28

questions 10, 11, 30

records 6, 9, 16, 20, 22
research 12
rulers 18

scales 18
scientific method 6, 8, 9, 12
sharing 25
supplies 28

thermometers 18
tools 18, 19, 26

variables 10

yardsticks 18